Street Murals

Volker Barthelmeh

Street Murals

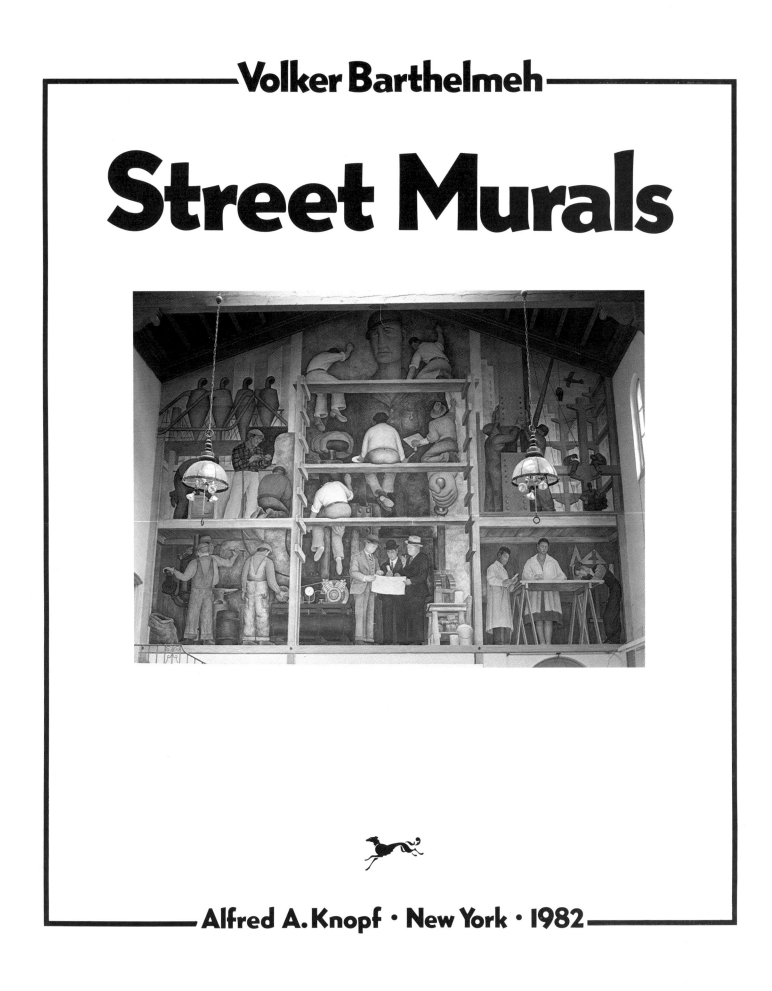

Alfred A. Knopf · New York · 1982

Overleaf illustration:
San Francisco, *California School of Fine Arts*
(San Francisco Art Institute) 1931, Diego Rivera

This is a Borzoi Book
Published by Alfred A. Knopf, Inc.

First American Edition
English translation Copyright © 1982 by Alfred A. Knopf, Inc.

All rights reserved under International and Pan-American Copyright Conven-
tions. Published in the United States by Alfred A. Knopf, Inc., New York, and
simultaneously in Canada by Random House of Canada Limited, Toronto.
Distributed by Random House, Inc., New York. Originally published in the
Federal Republic of Germany as WANDBILDER USA/WESTEUROPA by Verlag
Kiepenheuer & Witsch, Köln. Copyright © 1982 by Verlag Kiepenheuer &
Witsch, Köln

ISBN: 0-394-52783-6 hc
ISBN: 0-394-71196-3 pb

Library of Congress Catalog Card Number: 82-80836

In 1967, twenty-one black artists jointly painted a mural on a semi-abandoned building on the South Side of Chicago. A collage of painted portraits, photographs, and poems, it features black heroes and well-known personalities in politics, literature, religion, music, and sports. "This Wall was created to honor our Black Heroes, and to Beautify our Community," reads one inscription on the mural, which is an expression of the self-confidence that grew out of the "Black Power/Power to the People" civil rights movement. This "Wall of Respect" provided the impetus for the cooperative, community-based direction of the American mural movement, with blacks as well as other ethnic minorities (Chicanos, Puerto Ricans, Asians) seeing in it a visual means of expressing their cultural heritage, their solidarity, demands, needs, and desires.

The first murals appeared in New York City toward the end of the '60's at the instigation of architects and city planners. The abstract/geometric murals created by artists in the group City Walls (today's Public Arts Fund) were representative of other cities' intentions to bring "light and color into a grimy city."

While these murals were too often merely cosmetic, the mural movement developed much more imaginatively and in more depth in Los Angeles, San Francisco, and Berkeley, where it was influenced by the student movement and the counterculture. "In the spring of 1969, fellow artist Victor Henderson and I determined there was an alternative to the gallery-museum system of exhibiting art. Our idea was to paint large-scale exterior murals on available city walls. We cooperated on all aspects of the first works, choosing sites and ideas that we felt were right for large-scale work. The resulting paintings were complex and as completely crafted as any gallery works." This is how Terry Schoonhoven describes the mural movement in Venice, a section of Los Angeles. Later, he and Vic Henderson became known as the Los Angeles Fine Arts Squad. The movement's subsequent development toward the use of mural paintings to advertise companies and products was a natural one in view of the prevalence of billboard advertisements in the U.S.

Europe first learned about the American mural movement in the first half of the '70's—through publications. Mural art seemed a limitless medium, especially to those European countries who saw in it a counterweight to a shapeless, barren environment—but the results were decorative. Conversely, other murals criticized the origins of this very formlessness—poor planning, the demolition of houses, real-estate speculation, as, for example, in the Quartier Nord-Saint-Josse of Brussels, the Borough of Greenwich in London, the Bilk sector of Düsseldorf.

But murals also appeared in cities that were striving to expand the public offering of art. These were the result of fresh thinking by cultural-affairs departments and pressure from artists for meaningful, community-based art that would involve neighborhoods and groups of people who had never or seldom been in contact with art.

The wall paintings in Portugal, Spain, Italy, and Sardinia were fundamentally different. More closely related to graffiti, the Portuguese and Spanish murals were political posters which, like the murals created in Chile under Allende, reflected social unrest and change. Italian murals were either symbols of political protest (e.g., against poor housing conditions and urban planning in Rome) or a means of expression for fringe groups, such as the "indiani metropolitani" in Bologna. On the other hand, a mural covering the walls of an entire village in Sardinia tells of the social conditions and problems of the villagers.

The mural movement of the '60's in the States and in Europe brought about a renewed interest in its predecessors: the Mexican murals and the wall paintings that were created in the States under the New Deal.

The Mexican mural movement, which began following the Mexican Revolution (1910–1920), built on the fresco techniques of classical painters like Giotto and Michelangelo. After an experimental phase, it focused on social concerns—often the history of Mexico. "Mural art broke out of the rut into which painting had sunk. It swept away many prejudices and contributed a fresh perspective on social problems," noted José Clemente Orozco in his autobiography. Orozco later became known as one of "los tres grandes" of Mexican art; the other two were Diego Rivera and David Alfaro Siqueiros. In the '30's, these three artists also executed several commissions in the States; one, a Rivera mural in New York City's Rockefeller Center, was destroyed in February 1934, before it could be completed, because it portrayed Lenin.

The development of mural art in Mexico, together with the murals Orozco, Rivera, and Siqueiros created in the States in the '30's, provided the impetus for the New Deal art projects that were designed to support artists. Under the auspices of the most wide-ranging art program of the New Deal (the Federal Arts Program of the WPA),

over 2,500 wall paintings were created in offices, schools, hospitals, and libraries. For the first time in history, this art form, freed from its traditional artistic constraints, became popular in the United States.

Private initiative and financial support from businesspeople, companies, and private foundations played a substantial role in the start and continuation of the mural movement both in the United States and Europe.

With aid from state arts councils and the National Endowment for the Arts, mural art in America was soon able to expand into other programs, such as "Summerthing," the "Inner City Mural Program," and mural workshops. In Western Europe, mural paintings were created under the auspices of municipal authorities, such as the *Kultur- und Bausenate* (Bremen, Berlin), the *Rotterdamse Kunststichting* (Rotterdam), the Tower Hamlets Arts Committee of the Greater London Arts Association (London), the Arts Council of Great Britain, and *la municipalité de Grenoble* (Grenoble).

Eva and James Cockroft and John Weber described the collective character of mural art in their book, *Toward a People's Art*: "The murals were often executed by groups of artists or are designed and executed by non-professional local residents led by an artist." Examples of this type of collaborative effort are the murals of the Chicago Mural Group (21–23), and the New York Cityarts Workshop (14–17). Active involvement of local residents is also reflected in the London examples of the Greenwich Mural Workshop (78) and the Wadsworth Arts Resource Project of Brian Barnes, "The Seaside Picture" (76). A day's outing to Southend was specially arranged so that a group of people could be photographed for this mural. The finished mural, which Brian Barnes executed with the help of twenty local-people, contains sixty-four figures, all of which are faithful portrayals. To quote Brian Barnes about the creation of the mural: "The most impressive

way of people being involved in art is undoubtedly through mural painting. After lengthy discussions with local people as to the content of the image, the wall is prepared and squared-up. Then, from a scale design, I draw the image on the wall with charcoal, and people of all ages set to painting in the area. Depending on their manual dexterity, they paint what they can. If it's only background, color, or portraits, all can be proud of the finished picture." Local involvement is also evident in the mural paintings of Ray Walker (77) and the Art Workers Co-Operative (73). On the other hand, community-based murals are still a rarity in West Germany. Eckart Keller and Sönke Nissen portray forty-two people of a Hamburg neighborhood (86). They describe their personal motivation as follows: "We start from a need to create art not only for the arts establishment, but to extend its reach by working with groups of people who are not usually interested in art." In Oldenburg, local residents not only served as models, they also helped paint their own mural under the direction of Eckhart Haisch (95). It was the visual presentation of a communal feast that was painted after the feast had actually taken place. A mural in Bremen (93) that makes reference to the hundred-year history of its part of town was completed only after historical research and interviews with local people. This Bremen mural forms the link to other wall paintings which, while not directly connected with local residents, still mirror social events. They cover:
• historical developments and events (24, 43, 61, 92, 115)
• areas in the city (74, 81, 97, 118), schools (19), and businesses (63, 108)
• suppression of free speech (119) and threats to peace (75)
• the political situation in Central and South America (20, 62, 80, 109)

All these murals clearly demonstrate a conscious attempt on the part of the artists not to separate their art from the problems of the society in which they live.

To create only murals that are community based would, however, be as one-sided as following the theory of functional art. To claim that mural art effects lasting change would be an overstatement which would ignore the effects of social conditioning. It is, after all, hard to believe that a mural will transmit lasting cultural pride or even dignity to the many people living a desolate, marginal existence in urban ghettos, especially in the U.S. Even the community-building process of jointly creating a mural seldom has a lasting effect, since the concept of neighborhood or community is no longer valid in many cities.

On the other hand, to look only for substantive murals would disregard the expectations of a large part of the population for art that has meaning but is also enjoyable to look at. Expectations that today's artists rarely or never take into account. In my opinion, these expectations are not really answered by the much-quoted contention that a work of art can only exist as a work of art for the person able to possess—i.e., to decode—it. This is at best an attempt at mystification on the part of the artist and the art expert. It is, however, an incontrovertible fact that some individuals are barred access to art as a result of differences in social conditioning (e.g., family, school, profession).

The opinion "Art and life are one entity," which Robert Henri advanced at the beginning of this century, will probably remain a Utopian ideal. Nevertheless, mural art can offer an excellent opportunity to reduce the distance between art and everyday life.

Special thanks are due to all those whose help and cooperation have contributed to this photo book.   V.B.

Notes to individual murals (numbers are references to pages):

14–15 The painting was done by community artists under the direction of Alan Okada. This type of wall painting is what Cityarts Workshop calls "artist designed murals." After consultation with co-sponsors and neighborhood residents, the artist or team of artists develops a mural design which is then presented to the community for comment. The mural is painted with the participation of a community crew and/or teenage apprentices, who are usually art students.

16 The mural was painted by teenagers (Youth Mural) under the direction of Tomie Arai. It is one of the so-called "artist catalyst murals," where the artist works with a group of 10 to 20 participants—who may be teenagers or young adults, but also children, senior citizens, or residents of a therapeutic community—who usually have no artistic training. Participants determine the theme of the mural, contribute design elements, and participate in all aspects of wall preparation and painting.

17 Youth Mural. Director: Vivian Linares/Manny Vega.

20 Part of a collective antiwar mural. Marcos Raya dedicated it to "the People of Central and South America in their struggle for social, political, and economic independence."

21 Artists and residents of the community.

23 Partial view.

26 Besides the artists named, youth trainees and volunteers from the community helped with the mural. In addition to tremendous community support from local businesses, the project was funded by the Department of Housing and Urban Development (HUD) and the Walworth County CETA program.

The mural combines painting with hand-molded concrete relief sculpture. The figures to the right of the mill wheel depict three historical eras: Indian, early settlers, and contemporary; they represent the water that turns the wheel of change. The figures to the left of the wheel are taking what is already built to form the future. Photo: Caryl Yasko.

30 The mural title alludes to Locust Street's former name, Automobile Row, because of its concentration of car dealers and spare-parts manufacturers.

31 Blue Sky is the artistic pseudonym of Warren Honson.

32 Wall painting for a company that rents uniforms.

33 In addition to Zara Kriegstein, director, and Gilberto Guzman, the following also painted the mural: Rosemary Stearns, John Sandford, Cassandra Harris, David Bradley, and Frederico M. Vigil. A plaque states: "This mural is intended to bridge the gap between art and people. An international collaboration of artists, reviving mural art."

36 Section of mural "Monarch Bridal and Tuxedo."

37 The mural depicts the actress Lilian Bronson, who played in the "Perry Mason" TV series for many years.

38 Jan Clayton, familiar for her role as the mother in the '50's TV series "Lassie," represents the Virgin Mary here: in the center is Clayton Moore ("The Lone Ranger") as God, and on the right, Billy Gray, who played the son in "Father Knows Best," as Christ.

39 Here Kent Twitchell portrayed six Los Angeles artists: (from left to right) Marta Chaffee Stang, Alonzo Davis, Paul Czirban, Oliver Nowlin, Eloy Torrez, and Waynna Kato.

40 Photos made in April and September 1981 record stages in the development of a portrait of the artist Ed Ruscha.

41 Director: Josefina Quezada. Others involved in the painting were: Thelma Heavilin Sánchez, Susan Valdéz Torres, Rosa Q. Quezada, Patricia Rivera, Vivian Sánchez, and Herlinda Bustamanta.

42 One of three murals at Soto Street and Brooklyn Avenue, which were painted by fifteen people.

43 Partial views. Project direction: Judy Baka, Diane Ferrari, Leo Jauregui, Andrew Manning, Bea Plessner (supervisors), and 34 teenagers. Funded by the Project Heavy San Fernando Valley District. From 1976–80, the history of California took shape in three sections along a 2,600-foot-long wall. Altogether, 140 teenagers took part in the whole painting.

44 Partial view.

45 Section. With the collaboration of David Gatchel, Samuel Myung, and Marcia Alvarez.

46 With the collaboration of Chris Schlesinger, Mike Silva.

49 Photo: Terry Schoonhoven.

50 Section. Design: Jane Golden. Execution: Jane Golden, Barbara Stoll.

51 Section.

53 Partial view.

54 Partial views. The painting on the exterior walls of the meat-packing plant was started by Les Grimes in 1957. In 1968, while working on the scaffolding, he fell to his death. Arno Jordan, who continued the project, is currently responsible for regular upkeep of the painting.

55 Section. After the mural (which was movable) was taken down at the De Young Museum in Golden Gate Park, it found a new home in Fort Mason in 1980.

56 Partial views.

59 Further collaborators: Urania M. Lugo, Tricia Betancourt, Janet M. Lugo, Francine M. Theilen, and Kym Sitea.

61 Section.

62 Homage to Victor Jara, Chile's most popular folk singer, who was tortured to death in the International Stadium in Santiago after the Chilean coup. Jara's face, his arm, and the birds over the entrance to La Pena Center are three-dimensional.

63 Partial view.

65 Partial view. Freeway underpass.

66 Partial view.

68–69 Photos: Graham Cooper/Doug Sargent, London.

70 A local brewery underwrote costs of the mural, which was painted by a group.

71 Ken White painted this mural, assisted by art students from the College, Swindon. Depicted here are some Swindon residents whose fame has far exceeded that of the town—e.g., Diana Dors, Desmond Morris, and Gilbert O'Sullivan.

73 Jones and Barber were commissioned to do this mural by the Camden Council Planning Department. The artists' basic premise was to create art for and with local residents, paying special attention to themes of particular import to them. The Borough of Camden—like other parts of London—has been particularly affected by rampant private land speculation, which destroys old urban structures to make way for corporate high-rises.

74 The Covent Garden mural commemorates the successful efforts of local residents to create a small garden on this spot.

77 Partial view. The richly illustrated mural by Ray Walker is in Spitalfields, in London's East End. Traditionally, the garment industry has been the most important industry of the East End, heavily concentrated in Whitechapel and Bricklane. Many immigrants live and work in this section, largely from India, but particularly from Bangladesh. The mural depicts this neighborhood with all its social conditions, problems, and expectations.

78 Directors: Stephen Lobb, Carol Kenna.

80 The artists' group El Frente (The Front) consists of six Chilean exiles. Funded by the Senator für kulturelle Angelegenheiten.

81 Sponsored by the (Berlin) Abteilung Stadterneuerung/Modernisierung.

83 Painted on the courtyard wall of a house in Berlin-Charlottenburg.

84 Design acquired in the competition Art in Urban Space. Beneath the mural is a quote, in German and in Turkish, from the Turkish poet Nazim Hikmet, which provided the concept for the mural: "Life, / individual and free as a tree, /comradely as a forest, / is our desire."

85 Collective mural on a squatter's house in Berlin-Kreuzberg.

86 Special city funds for Kultur im Stadtteil were made available for this local mural. The design, with its portraits of 42 local residents who had previously been photographed, was actually painted by Keller and Nissen aided by a close-knit group of painters and illustrators.

89 Mural for a meat company.

90 With the collaboration of H. Streich. The landscape panels visible on the left of the painted café interior are also the subject of two other murals in the immediate vicinity. The underlying theme of all three murals was "urban encroachment and reclamation of the countryside by the people." With his design, the artist was trying to criticize the reclamation project by spelling out that the rural reclamation only existed on panels stuck inside a room.

91 Partial views.

92 Partial view.

93 Partial view. The hundred-year history of this part of Bremen (closely tied to Germany's changing history) is portrayed on three sides of a bunker—its transition from a small fishing village around the turn of the century to a working-class neighborhood that bore the strong stamp of the tradition-laden Actiengesellschaft Weser, Bremen's largest docks. The mural, developed in 1976–77 as a project of the Bremen Hochschule für Gestaltung, was based on current and historical research, including both written and pictorial sources and eyewitness accounts.

94 With the collaboration of Thomas Hartmann, Gerd Lüssen, and Jürgen Schmiedekampf.

95 The impetus for this mural was a street festival, "A Feast for Oldenburg," to which every resident brought something to eat and drink. The communal table where everyone sat, ate and talked, laughed and gestured together, provided the photographic model for the mural. Eckhart Haisch and other residents then worked out the final design, painted on the wall, using many snapshots and self-portraits. Conceived under the auspices of the Oldenburg Mural Symposium in the summer of 1981.

96 Done under the auspices of the Düsseldorf Film Festival 1980. Wall space was provided by the organization Neue Heimat Nordrhein-Westfalen.

97 The wall painting was the joint concept of the Düsseldorf Mural Group and the citizens' action group Save Bilk. Materials were paid for by contributions and the mural group worked without recompense.

99 The mural was created in October 1980, during the Congress of German Art Educators. The sailing-ship motif is modeled on the historical *Mayflower*. The wall painting, which 50 art teachers completed in just two days on the fire wall of an old firehouse, represents their attempt to motivate the congress along more practically oriented lines, and to underline their support for the local citizens' movement to turn the firehouse into a cultural center.

101 Erich Grams, a former miner in early retirement, painted the entire outside and inside of his house. As a result of a legal suit in which the owner of the building tried to claim compensation for "defacement," the painting was officially upgraded to "naive art" worthy of preservation.

108 Three-dimensional wall design.

110 Mural in a playground in Amsterdam.

113 At the invitation of the French cultural ministry, the Los Angeles Fine Arts Squad painted a mural in the fairgrounds, Parc Floral in Vincennes, for the 1971 Biennale. After 1977, it was no longer there. Photo: Terry Schoonhoven.

114 Section. Another temporary mural. In 1981, a new building was erected right up against this wall.

115 This mural was produced for a new union building Grenoble-Isère and funded by the city of Grenoble. The approximately 60 posters are painted onto the wall with most of the texts screened directly. The poster originals are authentic, discovered by the artist in the Grenoble city archives and in the union files. They cover a period from the end of the last century right up to the present, and relate to such national events as the popular front (1936) and May 1968. The two larger figures are reminiscent of the personal work of Ernest Pignon Ernest as represented in his poster show Intervention/Images, Paris, 1971, and Grenoble, 1976–77. Photo: Ernest Pignon Ernest.

118–19 Three of the many murals to be found along the Blvd. Emile Jacqmain in the Nord-Saint-Josse quarter of Brussels. The murals are on the walls of houses still standing, in an area where the homes of some 10,000 people were razed for a planned complex of eight high-rise buildings (Plan Manhattan). A Comité d'Action du Quartier Nord-Saint-Josse initiated the murals in order to improve the look of the remaining old houses and to bolster the survivors' morale. The murals, partly decorative and partly substantive, were made possible by corporate aid, especially from a local electrical firm, Sirtaine/François du Cugnac, and local and state authorities, as well as by pledges from volunteers. Meanwhile, Plan Manhattan—only one high-rise tower has been constructed—has been reduced in scope.

USA

New York City, South St. & Peck Slip. 1978. Design: Richard Haas. Public Art Fund/City Walls.

New York City, West 27th St. 1976. Design: Hugh Kepets. City Walls.

New York City, Madison & Pike St. 1974. ›Chi Lai/Arriva/Rise Up‹. Cityarts Workshop.

New York City, Delancey & Forsyth St. 1975. ›Seeds for Progressive Change‹. Cityarts Workshop.

New York City, Hester & Bowery St. 1977. ›Wall of Respect for the Working People of Chinatown‹. Cityarts Workshop.

New York City, East 103 rd. St. 1980. ›Unidos Venceremos‹. Cityarts Workshop.

Chicago, North La Salle. 1980. ›Homage to the Chicago School of Architecture‹. Design: Richard Haas.

Chicago, Lake Park Ave. 1980. Astrid Fuller.

Chicago, Western & 18th St. 1980. Marcos Raya.

Chicago, Fullerton & Washtenaw St. 1976. ›Tilt‹. John Weber/Connie Marek/Janek Kokot. Chicago Mural Group.

Chicago, 40th St. & Michigan Ave. Elliott Don Nelley Youth Center. 1980. ›Another Times Voice Remembers My Passion's Humanity‹. Calvin Jones/Mitchell Caton. Chicago Mural Group.

Chicago, West Ogden Blvd. & Central Park Ave. Westside Association for Community Action Bldg. 1980. ›Ceremonies for Heritage Now‹. Calvin Jones/Mitchell Caton. Chicago Mural Group.

Chicago, South Wabash Ave. & 49th St. Amalgamated Meat Cutters Union Hall. 1974. ›History of the Packinghouse Worker‹. William Walker.

Lemont/Ill., Canal & Stephens St. 1975. ›Lemont Bicentennial Mural‹. Caryl Yasko.

Whitewater/Wis., Center St. 1980. ›Prairie Tillers‹. Caryl Yasko/Niki Glen/Frenchy Le Tendre/Steve Englund.

Detroit. Eastern Farmers Market. Design: Alex Pollock.

Cincinnati, West Fifth & Plum St. 1973. **Design: Tom Smith.**

St. Louis, Gravois St. 1977. ›Face of a Nation‹. On the Wall Productions (Sarah Linquist/Bob Fishbone).

St. Louis, Locust Blvd. & Leffingwell Ave. 1979. ›Car Heaven‹. On the Wall Productions (Sarah Linquist/Bob Fishbone).

Columbia/S. Car., Marion & Hampton St. 1975. ›Tunnelvision‹. Blue Sky.

Fort Worth, West Lancaster & Jennings St. 1973. Stuart Gentling.

Santa Fé, Guadalupe. New Mexiko State Records Center. 1980. ›Multi-Cultural-Mural‹. Design: Zara Kriegstein/Gilberto Guzman.

Compton/Cal., Wilmington Ave. & El Segundo Blvd. Willowbrook Jr. High School. 1979/1980.
Richard Wyatt.

Comptom/Cal., Wilmington Ave. & El Segundo Blvd. Willowbrook Jr. High School. 1979. Richard Wyatt.

Los Angeles, South Broadway. 1975. ›Bride and Groom‹. Kent Twitchell.

Los Angeles, Temple St. & Hollywood Freeway. 1974. ›The Old Woman of the Freeway‹.
Kent Twitchell. Inner City Mural Program.

Los Angeles, Carondelet St. & Wilshire Blvd. Otis Art Institute. 1978. ›Trinity‹. Kent Twitchell.

Torrance/Cal., Engracia Ave. Employment Development Department Bldg. 1979. ›Six L. A. Artists‹. Kent Twitchell.

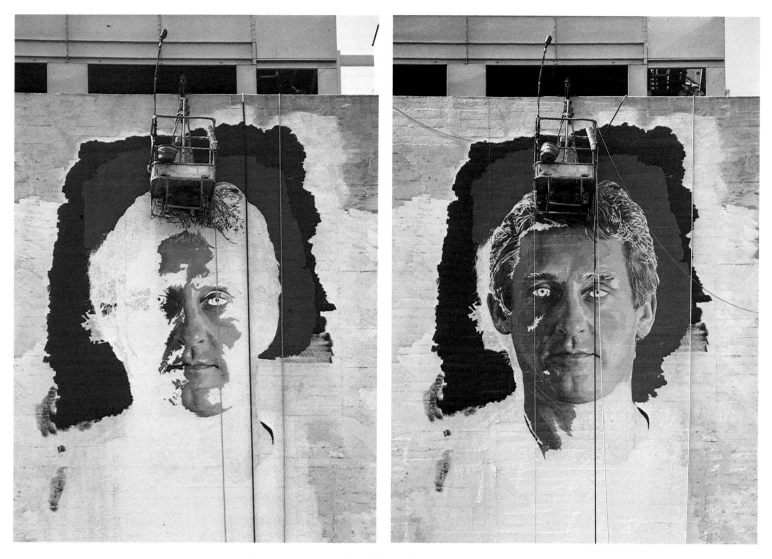

Los Angeles, South Hill St. 1981. ›Ed Ruscha Monument‹. Kent Twitchell.

Los Angeles, East Brooklyn Ave. & Hazard Ave. 1978. ›Read‹. Design: M. Teresa Chacón. Chicana Service Action Center.

Los Angeles, Soto St. & Brooklyn Ave. 1978. Design: John Valadez. Citywide Mural Project/ Public Art Center.

Los Angeles, Coldwater Canyon Ave. 1978. ›Tujanaga Wash Mural/History of California‹. Social and Public Art Resource Center (SPARC)/Citywide Mural Project.

Venice/Cal., Ocean Way & Windward Ave. 1978. ›Fall of Icarus‹. John Wehrle.

Venice/Cal., Beethoven St. & Venice Blvd. Randy Geraldi/Margaret Garcia. Citywide Mural Project.

Venice/Cal., Pacific Ave. & Market St. 1978. Joe Bravo.

Venice/Cal. Venice Pavilion. 1981. ›Venice on the Half Shell‹. R. Cronk.

Los Angeles, Butler Ave. & Santa Monica Blvd. 1971. ›The Isle of California‹. Los Angeles Fine Arts Squad.

Venice/Cal., Windward Ave. 1979. ›St. Charles Painting‹. Los Angeles Fine Arts Squad (Terry Schoonhoven).

Santa Monica, Ocean Park Blvd. & Main Street. 1976. Jane Golden. Citywide Mural Project.

Santa Monica, Lincoln & Ocean Park Blvd. 1978. Jane Golden.

Santa Monica, Ocean & Barnard Way. Arthur Mortimer.

Culver City/Cal., West Washington Blvd. & Purdue Ave. 1979. ›Moonscapes I/On the Tail of the Comet‹. Los Dos Streetscapers (Wayne Alaniz Healy/David Rivas Botello).

Vernon/Cal., Soto Blvd. & Vernon Ave. Farmer John Brand, Clougherty Meat Packing Co.
Les Grimes/Arno Jordan.

San Francisco. Fort Mason. 1976. ›Positively 4th Street‹. John Wehrle/John Rampley.

San Francisco, O'Farrell & Polk St. O'Farrell Theater. 1979. ›Oceania‹. Gary W. Graham/
Edgar Monroe/Lou Silva.

San Francisco, Frederick St. 1980. Carlos Marchiori.

San Francisco, Belvedere St. Earl Paltenghi Youth Center. 1977 ›The Spirit of Youth in America‹. Charles Lobdell.

San Francisco, Church St. Mission High School. 1980. Judy Jamerson.

San Francisco, 26th & Folsom St. LULAC Bldg. 1975. Gilberto Ramirez.

Berkeley/Cal., Haste St. & Telegraph Ave. 1976. ›A People's History of Telegraph Avenue‹. Osha Neumann/Daniel Galvez/Brian Thiele.

Berkeley/Cal., Prince St. & Shattuck Ave. La Pena Cultural Center. 1977. ›Song of Unity‹. Osha Neumann/Ray Patlan/Brian Thiele/Anna de Leon.

Berkeley/Cal., Sacramento St. & University Ave. Co-op Credit Union Bldg. 1977. ›Winds of Change‹. Osha Neumann/Daniel Galvez/Brian Thiele.

Berkeley/Cal., Telegraph Ave. Willard Jr. High School. 1980. ›Intersections‹. Osha Neumann/Daniel Galvez/Brian Thiele.

Berkeley, Claremont Ave. 1979. ›Oceanus‹. Vista College. Instructor: Gary W. Graham. Design: Edgar Monroe/Lou Silva.

Albany/Cal., Gilman St. & Santa Fe Ave. 1979. ›ancisco‹. John Wehrle.

England

Exeter, New Bridge St. 1980. ›Street Fair‹. Andrew Stacey.

Coventry, Adelaide St. Lanchester Polytechnic. 1977. ›Patience is a Virtue‹. Colin Slater.

Swindon. 1976. ›King Class Locomotive passing through Swindon Railway Works‹. Thamesdown Community Arts Project.

Swindon, Union St. 1979. ›Swindon Personalities‹. Ken White. Thamesdown Community Arts Project.

Swindon, Fleming Way. 1976. ›The Golden Lion Bridge‹. Ken White. Thamesdown Community Arts Project.

London, Tottenham Court Road. 1980. ›Fitzrovia Community Mural‹. Art Workers Co-Operative (Mike Jones/Simon Barber).

London, Earlham St. 1977. ›Garden Mural‹. Stephen Pussey.

London, Coldharbour Lane. 1981. ›Nuclear Dawn‹. Brian Barnes/Dale Mc Crea. WARP (Wandsworth Arts Resource Project).

London, Thessaly & Wandsworth Road. 1979. ›The Seaside Picture‹. Brian Barnes. WARP (Wandsworth Arts Resource Project).

London, Chicksand St. & Bricklane. 1980. ›Promised Land‹. Ray Walker. THAP (Tower Hamlets Arts Project).

London, Floyd Road. 1976. ›Floyd Road‹. Greenwich Mural Workshop.

Bundesrepublik
Deutschland

Berlin, Kochstraße. 1979. ›Hoffnung der Chilenen‹. Künstlergruppe ›El Frente‹.

Berlin, Pritzwalker Straße. 1979. Künstlergruppe RATGEB (Paul Blankenburg/Werner Brunner/Werner Steinbrecher).

81

Berlin, Lietzenseeufer. Seehof-Hotel. 1979. Gert Neuhaus.

Berlin, Zillestraße. 1979. Gert Neuhaus.

Berlin, Gneisenau & Schleiermacherstraße. 1980. Akbar Behkalam.

Berlin, Anhalter Straße. KuKuCK (Kunst- und Kultur-Centrum). 1981.

Hamburg, Vereins- & Margaretenstraße. 1979. Eckart Keller/Sönke Nissen.

Bremen, Drakenburger Straße & Fleetrade. 1981. Jörn Peter Dirx.

Bremen, Rembertiring. 1976. Peter K. F. Krüger. ›Kunst im öffentlichen Raum‹.

Bremen, Zum Sebaldsbrücker Bahnhof. 1978. Peter K. F. Krüger.

Bremen, Graubündener & Züricher & Tessiner Straße. 1979. Peter K. F. Krüger.
›Kunst im öffentlichen Raum‹.

Bremen, Mahndorfer Bahnhof. Bürgerhaus. 1979. ›Ein Dorf stellt sich vor‹. Ilona C. Krämer.
›Kunst im öffentlichen Raum‹.

Bremen, Neukirchstraße. 1980. ›Fortschritt und Stillstand – aus der Geschichte der Kleinbahn Jan Reiners‹. Jürgen Schmiedekampf. ›Kunst im öffentlichen Raum‹.

Bremen, Pastorenweg & Grasberger Straße. 1978. ›Geschichte des Stadtteils Gröpelingen 1878–1978‹. Jürgen Waller mit Studenten und Studentinnen der Hochschule für Gestaltung Bremen. ›Kunst im öffentlichen Raum‹.

Bremerhaven, Wursterstraße. 1980. ›Generationen‹. Marion Ubben. ›Kunst im öffentlichen Raum‹.

Oldenburg, Beowulfsweg. 1981. ›Ein Fressen für Oldenburg‹. Konzeption: Eckhart Haisch.

Düsseldorf, Von-Krüger-Straße. 1980. ›Marlene Dietrich und Spiderman‹. Wilhelm Moser.

Düsseldorf, Martinstraße. 1980. Düsseldorfer Wandmalgruppe.

Düsseldorf, Hellweg. 1979/1980. Düsseldorfer Wandmalgruppe.

Köln, Sudermannsplatz. Bürgerzentrum Alte Feuerwache. 1980. ›Die Hoffnung‹.

Köln, Geibelstraße. 1979. Wolfgang Ackermann/Günter Göttker.

Karlshausen/Eifel. Erich Grams.

Wuppertal, Sonnborner Straße & Sonnborner Ufer. 1981. Hans-Günther Obermaier.

Ulm. Neue Universität. 1977. Design: Universitätsbauamt Ulm.

Nederland

Utrecht, Adelaarstraat. 1980. Hans van der Plas.

Rotterdam, Haagseveer. 1976. ›Touwtje Springend Meisje‹. Co Westerik. Rotterdamse Kunststichting.

Rotterdam, Oude Binnenweg. 1976. Louis-Anne Looyschelder. Rotterdamse Kunststichting.

Rotterdam, Klostraat & Putselaan. 1979. ›Groeten uit Rotterdam‹. Hans Citroen. Rotterdamse Kunststichting.

Alkmaar, Scheteldoekshaven. 1979. ›Chili Vrij‹. Brigada Elmo Catalan.

Amsterdam, Zeedijk. 1979. Hans Hamers.

France

Le Vaudreuil/ville nouvelle, Route de Louviers & Voie de l'Aronde. 1977. ›Chenil‹. Henri Cueco.

Paris/Vincennes. Parc Floral. 1971. ›Hippie Knowhow‹. Los Angeles Fine Arts Squad.

Paris, Rue Rambuteau/Forum des Halles. 1979. ›Le piéton des Halles‹. Fabio Rieti.

Grenoble. Bourse de Travail. 1979. Ernest Pignon Ernest.

Paris, Rue Clisson. 1980. ›Jean Sebastien Bach‹. Fabio Rieti.

116

Belgique

Brüssel, bd. Emile Jacqmain prolongé & Rue de la Bienfaisance. 1978/1979. ›Le Café dans la ville‹. Véronique Thomas/Peter Schuppisser. ›La Grande Place se réflétant dans les vitres du WTC‹. Serge de Backer.

Brüssel, bd. Emile Jacqmain prolongé. 1979. ›Les droits de l'homme‹. Paul Van Nyverseel.

Brüssel, Rue Bernaerts. 1975. Paul de Gobert.

120